A Rainbow for My Daddy

Written by Tiffany Correa Castro

Illustrated by Ethan Roffler

ISBN: 978-0-578-99700-1

Illustrations and layout by Stories Untold LLC.

To: _____

From: _____

Date: _____

Dedication

For Sofia Grace and Eva Angeline,

When I saw darkness, you showed me light. When I was unable to breathe, you taught me how. When I thought this world had no happiness, you made me smile. You are my sunshine, my every breath, my world. The angels danced the day you were born teaching me how to dance again. You are a beautiful reminder of the love created and that a part of him lives on in each of you. What a gift to be given. My wish for you is to always feel the presence of your guardian angel's light. Call upon him in celebration. Call upon him in sadness. He will never leave your side. You will never be alone.

Mom

Hay Amores JAC

It is quite a view indeed.

One day my daddy went away.

Where did he go? I want to play!

He was here with us and then
suddenly gone.

How did this happen? What
went wrong?

Mommy was sad. I thought it was me.

Then she told me how this had come to be.

Daddy was gone and was not
coming home.

I couldn't understand. Why were we
all alone?

"His body broke, honey. He didn't need it anymore,"

Mommy said, staring down at the floor.

"Just like a butterfly that loses its cocoon,

Daddy's soul went to Heaven, up past the moon."

"A soul? What's that? I need to know.

Heaven? Where is it and when can I go?

Can I get there by plane, by car or by bus?

Oh, why did my daddy have to leave us?"

"Our souls are what makes us who we are.

Heaven is a place that is really far.

It's farther than the planets and past outer space,"

Mommy explained while caressing my face.

"You can only go to Heaven once you die.

You cannot visit," she said with a sigh.

"Why did he die? I don't understand."

"It's not up to us," she said. "There's a bigger plan."

Now Mommy has to work more than ever before.

I wish that Daddy would just walk through the door.

Sometimes I feel **angry**, **lonely**, and **sad**.

It's just not fair that I don't have my dad.

Mommy says, "Don't worry. What you feel is okay.

Sometimes I feel exactly the same way."

But this is so **hard**. What can I do?

I **miss** the daddy I once knew.

Mommy says I can **yell**, **scream**, **cry** and **pout**.

I feel better after I let it all out.

There are days when we talk about **worries** and **fears**.

After we're done we wipe away tears.

Other times when we talk we have **smiles** on our faces.

We think of puppy dog kisses, adventures to faraway places,

Climbing tall trees, blooming flowers, and the warm sun,

Delicious ice cream, playing ball and hitting a **homerun!**

Hearing a bluebird sing a pretty song, and **giggling** when Mommy tickles my tum.

Building sandcastles at the beach in the sand.

Selling lemonade at my very own stand.

Riding bikes with my sis, playing games with my mom.

Mommy says I shouldn't forget to have **fun**.

We end with a **hug** that makes me
feel better.

My **heart** is filled with **love** whenever
we're together.

I smile at **rainbows**. They're a sign
from above,

Sent down from Heaven as a symbol
of **love**.

My family is different since we lost my **dad**,

But I know now that not every day will be sad.

There is so much in store for me to do and see.

I am **special** and uniquely me.

I am **blessed** and I am **loved**

From this **Earth** and from **above**.

The End

ABOUT THE AUTHOR

 Tiffany Correa Castro, author of A Rainbow for My Daddy, a children's bereavement book, was born and raised in San Jose, California.
A Rainbow for My Daddy was inspired by the sudden, tragic, and life-altering death of her husband. With a toddler and another baby on the way, she found her strength and resiliency in her family, friends, and faith. Mrs. Correa Castro received her Bachelor's degree in Spanish, with a minor in Portuguese, from San Diego State University and is a member of the Society of Children's Book Writers and Illustrators.

She has made a lifelong career as a New York-and San Francisco-based flight attendant for a major airline. When she's not flying the friendly skies, she enjoys spending time with her family and friends, jogging, skiing, traveling, and learning foreign languages. She currently resides in Idaho with her two daughters, husband, the family chihuahua Leila, and Maximilian the chameleon.

ABOUT THE ILLUSTRATOR AND CO.

 As a kid who grew up in the rainy Seattle area, Ethan Roffler spent a lot of time stuck inside plotting world domination and the downfall of his siblings. He learned at an early age to embrace his creative side. As Ethan grew older, his love for art grew as well. He remembers his excitement when the local newspaper published some of the comic strips he created. He wanted to always hold on to that feeling. As a freelance artist Ethan got to participate in all sorts of creative projects. Although each project is dear to him, Ethan holds illustrating children's books very close to his heart, even more now that he has two little munchkins of his own.

Ethan founded Stories Untold in 2017 when he and his wife, Crystal, first entered into the world of children's books. After working with several authors, they saw how truly difficult, expensive, and intimidating it was for new authors to create and try to publish their books.

The Roffler's became determined to find a solution for authors to make their dream of being a "published author" much more attainable. To accomplish this, they put together a team of amazing people who felt the same way they did. This team intends to make the book creation process fun, affordable, and less stressful.

Local Recources

USA

https://Childrengrieve.org
https://Allinahealth.org
https://www.Widowcare.org
https://healgrief.org
National Hospice and Palliative Care Organization
americanwidowproject.org
American Widow Project Serving Military Families
Suicide Prevention Hotline 800-273-8255

Canada

www.grievingchildrenlighthouse.org
https://Hearthousehospice.com
https://Myraskids.ca
https://www.Circleofcare.com
Bereavement support 416-635-2860 ext 271

United Kingdom

https://widowedandyoung.org.UK
WAY -Widowed and Young Foundation
https://www.nhs.uk
https://www.thegoodgrieftrust.org or
call 0800 2600 400
Our Frontline: Free and Confidential 24/7
Mental Health, Social Care,
and Emergency Services. 0300 303 4434
https://childhoodbereavementnetwork.org.uk

Australia

https://www.grief.org.au
https://Griefline.org.au or call 1 300 845 745
0600-Midnight AEST, 7 days a week
https://Bereavement.org.au
https://www.lifeline.org.au
Suicide Prevention Call 13 11 14
https://Childhoodgrief.org.au

New Zealand

https://www.griefcentre.org.nz
https://kidslink.co.nz
Trauma and Grief Support for Children and Parents
https://www.cancer.org.nz
https://mentalhealth.org.nz

Additional Resources

I'm Grieving as Fast as I Can By: Linda Feinberg
Healing a Spouse's Grieving Heart By: Alan D Wolfelt
Widow to Widow By: Genevieve Davis Ginsburg

How I Feel Today:

How I Feel Today:

How I Feel Today:

How I Feel Today:

How I Feel Today:

How I Feel Today:

How I Feel Today:

How I Feel Today:

Although he is far away, forever in my heart he will stay...

CPSIA information can be obtained
at www.ICGtesting.com
Printed in the USA
LVHW070955200422
716460LV00033BA/196